1070L

Ruth Tenzer Feldman

Lerner Publications Company
Minneapolis

For Ben and Keith
And in memory of Addie Mae Collins, Denise McNair,
Carole Robertson, and Cynthia Wesley—justice, justice
shall you pursue.

A&E and **BIOGRAPHY** are trademarks of the A&E Television
Networks, registered in the United States and other countries.

Some of the people profiled in this series have also been featured in
A&E's acclaimed BIOGRAPHY series, which is available on videocassette
from A&E Home Video. Call 1-800-423-1212 to order.

Lerner Publications Company
A division of Lerner Publishing Group
241 First Avenue North
Minneapolis, MN 55401 U.S.A.

Website address: www.lernerbooks.com

Library of Congress Cataloging-in-Publication Data

Feldman, Ruth Tenzer.
  Thurgood Marshall / by Ruth Tenzer Feldman.
    p.   cm. — (A&E biography)
Includes bibliographical references and index.
  ISBN 0-8225-4989-1 (lib. bdg.: alk. paper)
    1. Marshall, Thurgood, 1908–1993—Juvenile literature. 2. Judges—
United States—Biography—Juvenile literature. 3. Afro-American judges—
United States—Biography—Juvenile literature. 4. United States—
Supreme Court—Biography—Juvenile literature. [1. Marshall, Thurgood,
1908–1993. 2. Lawyers. 3. Judges. 4. United States—Supreme Court—
Biography. 5. Afro-Americans—Biography.] I. Title. II. Series.
KF8745.M34 F45 2001
347.73'2634—dc21   00-009500

Manufactured in the United States of America
1 2 3 4 5 6 – JR – 06 05 04 03 02 01

CONTENTS

In the South, where Thurgood Marshall lived, whites-only signs like this one were common in the mid-twentieth century.

INTRODUCTION

Thurgood Marshall liked parties, but not the one planned for him on November 18, 1946, in Columbia, Tennessee. He recalled being held in a police car as law enforcement officers "carried me down toward the river. When we got [there] you could see the people for the party. By party, I mean lynch party." The white lynch mob waited for its chance to hang Thurgood, a black man.

Nine months before Thurgood's "party," James Stephenson, a nineteen-year-old black veteran of World War II, and his mother went to Billy Fleming's repair shop. They complained to Fleming, a white man, that he hadn't fixed their radio. Fleming slapped Mrs. Stephenson and pushed her out the door. James Stephenson punched Fleming, who fell through a plate-glass window. Fleming went to the hospital. The Stephensons went to jail.

That night, a mob of angry whites gathered in town. Sheriff J. J. Underwood worried that the mob might lynch the Stephensons. Lynch mobs weren't uncommon in the South. These mobs of citizens would take the law into their own hands and kill people accused or suspected of crimes, often before a trial had taken place. Most victims of lynchings in the twentieth century were black citizens, who usually were hung or burned to death. Sheriff Underwood didn't want that to happen to the Stephensons. He asked two black men to meet him by the jail's back door and smuggle the Stephensons out of town. Underwood prevented the lynching, but a riot ensued. The mob attacked Columbia's blacks, who had hunkered down in Mink Slide, the black business district. The blacks were armed and determined to protect themselves.

After the riot, state troopers wrecked the stores in Mink Slide, saying they were looking for hidden guns and ammunition. They arrested about one hundred blacks. Two Tennessee lawyers—a white man named Maurice Weaver and a black man named Z. Alexander Looby—were able to free all but about twenty-five men. Then Thurgood Marshall, the chief lawyer for the Legal Defense and Educational Fund of the National Association for the Advancement of Colored People (NAACP), came to town.

Hoping to ease tensions, Thurgood persuaded the Columbia judge to move the trial to another city. The judge moved the proceedings to Lawrenceburg, which didn't seem much friendlier toward blacks. A sign at the city line warned blacks, "NIGGER, READ AND RUN. DON'T LET THE SUN GO DOWN ON YOU HERE. IF YOU CAN'T READ, RUN ANYWAY."

Nearly all of the defendants (charged with inciting to riot and attempted murder) at the Lawrenceburg trial were found not guilty. Two defendants, however, were charged separately with the more serious crime of firing at state highway patrol officers and were tried in Columbia. One man was found not guilty; the other received a five-year sentence that was later reduced to ten months. On November 18, 1946, after the trial ended, Thurgood, Looby, Weaver, and a reporter named Harry Raymond left Columbia in Looby's car. They were on their way to Nashville, where they had stayed during the trial because they feared radical whites in Columbia would attack them if they stayed in the community.

Before the group traveled far, the Columbia police stopped them, ordered Thurgood and the others out of Looby's car, then searched the car for illegal liquor. When the police didn't find any liquor, Thurgood and his friends got back in their car, and Looby drove away.

The police stopped them again and arrested Thurgood, who had been riding in the back seat, for drunken driving. They wedged him into a police car between two men holding guns and told Thurgood's friends to leave. Then the car with Thurgood inside turned down a narrow dirt road leading to a secluded spot on the Duck River. Looby followed. "[The police] told Looby and the other guys to keep going the other way," Thurgood recalled. "Looby wouldn't go the other way. He was one brave man."

As they approached the river, Thurgood saw a mob of white men waiting by the water for the police car. He knew the mob was there to lynch him. But Looby and the others were still right behind him. The police officers were disturbed by the presence of Thurgood's friends as potential witnesses. To Thurgood's profound relief, the police car drove away from the mob without stopping.

But the ordeal wasn't over yet. Stopping back in town, the police ordered Thurgood to walk alone to a local judge's office. The street was nearly deserted because "everybody was down at the Duck River waiting for the party." Thurgood was suspicious, and he refused to go by himself. "You ain't going to shoot me in the back while [claiming I was] escaping—no way." So he and the police walked to the office together. Thurgood's friends watched every move.

The police told the elderly judge that they had arrested Thurgood for drunken driving. The judge said "You want to take my test? ... I've never had a drink in my life. I can smell liquor a mile off. You blow your breath on me." Thurgood blew, and the judge pronounced him sober. That instant the police vanished. Thurgood raced outside. His friends were gone. He ran to Mink Slide, where he found them with Columbia's black leaders. They quickly made plans to leave town undetected by the police or angry whites. Someone from town took Looby's car and drove away. Thurgood and his friends drove another car in a different direction. Just as they left, a group of whites drove up. They followed Looby's car, and when they found out Thurgood wasn't in it, they beat the driver so badly he required hospitalization.

When Thurgood finally reached Nashville, he reported

the incident to Attorney General Tom Clark. Clark investigated what had happened in Columbia, but no charges were ever filed against anyone for the "party" Thurgood had narrowly missed. Little had changed for African Americans in the South in the thirty-eight years since Thurgood's birth.

This photo of Thurgood Marshall was probably taken around July 1910, when he turned two.

Chapter **ONE**

BALTIMORE IN BLACK AND WHITE

THURGOOD MARSHALL WAS BORN JULY 2, 1908, in Baltimore, Maryland. His father, William Canfield Marshall, was a dining-car waiter on the Baltimore & Ohio (B&O) Railroad. His mother, Norma Williams Marshall, looked after Thurgood and his older brother, William Aubrey, whom the family called by his middle name.

In honor of his paternal grandfather, Thurgood was given two first names, Thorneygood and Thoroughgood, when he was born. When Thurgood's grandfather, a former slave, had joined the U.S. Army, he hadn't been sure what to call himself. So he signed up under both names and later wound up getting two sets of retirement checks. In time, grandson Marshall would decide he preferred the name Thoroughgood. In the second or third grade, he would shorten it to Thurgood.

When Thurgood was a toddler, the Marshalls moved to New York City and stayed with Norma Marshall's sister, Denmedia, and her husband. Thurgood's mother attended Columbia University's teachers college while Thurgood and Aubrey spent time with Aunt "Medi."

Thurgood was a timid child, with very light brown skin, wavy brown hair, and big brown eyes. He brought stray animals, and sometimes stray people, to the apartment and pleaded with his mother to feed them. Because of this kind behavior, his family nick-named him "Goody."

The Marshalls returned to Baltimore before Thurgood began school. William Marshall found work as the steward—a waiter—for the Gibson Island Country Club, a private club that blacks and Jews were not allowed to join. Most of Thurgood's extended family lived in Baltimore, and he spent a lot of time with them. Both sets of his grandparents owned grocery stores in Baltimore.

Thurgood's maternal grandmother, Mary Williams, was a teacher like his mother. She hoped Aubrey and Thurgood would one day become doctors or dentists, but she wanted to make sure they could always earn money. So Grandma Mary taught the boys how to cook, thinking there would always be jobs for black men as cooks. Thurgood enjoyed cooking so much

Thurgood's father and mother, William and Norma Marshall

that it became a lifelong hobby. He specialized in chocolate cake and Grandma Mary's crab soup.

Thurgood's maternal grandfather was Isaiah Olive Branch Williams, who served in the U.S. Navy before settling in Baltimore. Isaiah Williams gave each of his six children unusual names. Thurgood's mother was named after an opera titled *Norma*. Aunt Denmedia Marketa was named for the grocery store Williams owned on Denmeade Street. An uncle was named Fearless Mentor. Thurgood called Fearless "Uncle Fee," and the two spent a lot of time together. In fact, in 1914, Thurgood's family moved in with Uncle Fee and his wife for several years.

Both white and black middle-class families lived in Uncle Fee's neighborhood. The Hales, a white Jewish family who had a grocery store on the first floor of their house, lived next door. Sammy Hale and Thurgood were about the same age and became good friends. When Sammy began to work in his family's store, Thurgood got his first job there too. Seven-year-old Thurgood ran errands for ten cents a day plus all he could eat.

The Marshalls sometimes ate dinner with the Hales, which rarely happened then among black families and white families, even in Baltimore's integrated neighborhoods. Baltimore was a city stuck geographically and culturally between the North and the South. Thurgood called Baltimore "way up South." For generations, blacks had been able to own businesses and become professionals. However, during Thurgood's youth, blacks were not welcomed in many of Baltimore's stores, theaters, and restaurants. By state law, there were "white" and "colored" toilets on trains and steamships operating in Baltimore and throughout Maryland.

Since Sammy Hale was white and Thurgood black, they went to different elementary schools. Fights broke out between Thurgood's schoolmates and white children at a Catholic school two blocks away. Sometimes Thurgood was involved in these fights. In Thurgood's all-black elementary school on Division Street, "Goody" Marshall was anything but good. Since his mother taught at the same school, Thurgood figured her teacher friends would not flunk him. He acted silly in class, rarely studied, and generally drove his mother crazy.

Just before Thurgood started high school, the Marshalls left Uncle Fee's house and moved to a three-storied row house in a mostly black neighborhood. Aubrey studied hard and behaved himself. But Goody was another matter. "We lived on a respectable street, but behind us there were back alleys where the roughnecks and the tough kids hung out. When it was time for dinner, my mother used to go to the front door and call my older brother. Then she'd go to the back door and call me," he said. Norma Marshall tried to tame Thurgood a bit. At her insistence, he served as an altar boy at St. Katherine's Episcopal Church.

In 1921 Thurgood began attending the Colored High and Training School. The old building, which was renamed Frederick Douglass High School in 1923, had no library, cafeteria, or gym, but that didn't seem to bother Thurgood. He loved high school. He played football, led the debating team, served on the student council, and dated a lot of girls. Because Thurgood was tall and lanky, his classmates nicknamed him "Legs." Thurgood still acted so wild that Uncle Fee began to call him a bum.

William Marshall was the one who sparked Thurgood's interest in law. Thurgood's father never finished high school, but if he had continued his education, he might have made a good lawyer. He loved watching trials at the local courthouse whenever he could, and he often took Thurgood with him. He made sure Thurgood read the newspaper every day. During dinner, the Marshall men often debated, sometimes so loudly that neighbors complained. Thurgood once said that his father "never told me to become a lawyer. But he turned me into one by teaching me to argue, to prove every statement I made, and by challenging my logic on every point."

Thurgood's father also taught him to fight anyone who called him "nigger." Thurgood practiced that lesson at least once. While in high school, Thurgood

Thurgood graduated from Frederick Douglass High School in 1925.

worked for Mortimer Schoen, a Jewish man who made expensive hats for the richest people in Baltimore. At rush hour one evening, Thurgood awkwardly tried to board a trolley car while carrying a large stack of boxed hats. In boarding, he went ahead of a white woman. Suddenly a man grabbed him, told him never to step in front of a white woman, and called him "nigger." Thurgood dropped the boxes and started fighting. He was arrested. When he telephoned Schoen to tell him what had happened, Schoen paid Thurgood's bail, assured him he had done the right thing, and ignored the ruined hats.

Around this time, Thurgood suffered an even more humiliating experience. While in downtown Baltimore one Saturday, he needed to use a bathroom. Since blacks weren't allowed to use toilet facilities downtown, Thurgood took a trolley home. "And I did get almost in the house, when I ruined the front doorsteps," he said.

Thurgood graduated from high school in 1925, one semester early. Despite his wild behavior, he had earned a B average and a certificate for good attendance. Because of his wild behavior and poor study habits, Thurgood had also spent hours reading the document that would become the focus of his life's work. Whenever Thurgood acted up—which was often—the principal sent him to the school basement with orders to memorize portions of the United States Constitution.

The campus of Lincoln University during the late 1920s when Thurgood was a student. The university takes its name from President Abraham Lincoln.

Chapter **TWO**

LESSONS AT LINCOLN

As soon as **Thurgood finished high school,** he started working full time to earn money for college. Like his father before him, Thurgood worked as a dining-car waiter on the B&O Railroad. He quickly learned he was lucky just to have a job. When Thurgood found his uniform pants were too short and asked for a pair that fit better, the steward said, "Boy, we can get a man to fit the pants a lot easier than we can get the pants to fit the man. Why don't you just kinda scroonch down in 'em a little more?" Thurgood scroonched.

In September 1925, Thurgood and Aubrey left for Lincoln University, a small, all-male school in Oxford, Pennsylvania, about sixty miles from home. Lincoln's students were predominantly black. The faculty then was all white. Aubrey, who planned to go to medical school, was an honor roll student returning for his senior year. Thurgood, at seventeen, was a freshman eager to have fun.

Thurgood roomed with James Murphy, a friend whose family published Baltimore's *Afro-American* newspaper. He joined a fraternity and threw himself into the social life on campus. He loved to play cards, especially pinochle and poker, and he often joined in celebrations after football games. Thurgood formed the Weekend Club, whose members were not allowed to stay on campus on weekends unless one of Lincoln's athletic teams had a home game. Club members often took the train to Philadelphia, where blacks could enjoy restaurants, theaters, and nightclubs. Thurgood seldom studied, and he earned mediocre grades.

By sophomore year, Thurgood was a star on the debating team, the one academic activity that sparked his energy and showed his intelligence. He had become friends with Langston Hughes. Hughes had enrolled at Lincoln in 1926, when he was twenty-four and already a prominent poet, with regular invitations to artistic functions in Manhattan and ties to the NAACP.

Hughes helped Thurgood develop a greater awareness of racial issues. The mostly white town of Oxford, Pennsylvania, was north of the Mason-Dixon line, which had separated slave states from free states before the Civil War. But Oxford's movie theater re-

In this photo from 1926, Thurgood and fellow classmates sit on the steps of Lincoln University. Thurgood is the second from the right in the second row.

quired blacks to sit in the balcony. One night, several Lincoln students, including Thurgood, decided they had the right to sit anywhere, so they took seats on the main level. Thurgood later wrote to his father, "We found out that they only had one fat cop in the whole town, and they wouldn't have had the nerve or the room in the jail to arrest all of us. But the amazing thing was, when we were leaving . . . they didn't do anything, didn't say a thing, didn't even look at us—at least, as far as I know. I'm not sure I like being invisible, but maybe it's better than being put to shame and not able to respect yourself."

When Thurgood returned to campus, Langston Hughes urged him to get serious about protesting "Jim Crow." The term describes segregation laws and practices that oppress African Americans. The name "Jim Crow" is probably taken from a demeaning song-and-dance routine that became popular before the Civil War. Thurgood talked with his sociology teacher, Robert Labaree, about racial injustice in America. He read W. E. B. Du Bois's *The Souls of Black Folk* and his editorials in *The Crisis,* a magazine published by the NAACP. The NAACP had been founded by a group of blacks and whites about the time of Thurgood's birth and initially concentrated on preventing mob violence and lynchings. Thurgood began to focus less on fraternity pranks and more on issues the NAACP addressed.

During his sophomore and junior years at Lincoln, Thurgood continued to get passing grades without studying very hard. He did work hard, however, at debating team activities, reading a lot of books to prepare for debates. Debating was a natural extension of evenings at the Marshall home when Thurgood and Aubrey returned for visits. "My dad, my brother, and I had the most violent arguments about anything," Thurgood remembered later. "I guess we argued five nights out of seven at the dinner table. . . . I remember a neighbor of ours, Mrs. Hall, would tell her husband 'Ah, the boys are home' . . . [because] she could hear the arguments through the walls."

In the spring of 1928, Thurgood's education received a temporary setback. He and a few Lincoln friends hitched a ride from Baltimore to school, but the truck that picked them up broke down. They pushed it to a garage in Rising Sun, Maryland. While they waited for repairs, the local sheriff stopped by and told the mechanic he wanted "these niggers out of here before sundown." As soon as the truck was fixed, everyone climbed in—except Thurgood, who had wandered off. As the truck rolled along, Thurgood ran to catch up with it, jumped on, and severely injured himself when he collided with the tailgate. The injury required surgery and caused him to miss a semester of school.

When Thurgood returned to Lincoln, he worked harder at his studies. That same semester, Vivian Burey, a black student at the University of Pennsylvania, caught his complete attention socially. Nicknamed "Buster," Vivian had a sparkling, vivacious personality. The two quickly fell in love.

Uncle Fearless warned Buster that Thurgood was a bum, but she married him anyway, on September 4, 1929. They moved to a small apartment in Oxford. Thurgood finished his senior year, and Buster worked as a secretary.

Buster told Thurgood again and again that he could make a difference in society. Thurgood's experiences— trips to the courthouse with his father, hours in the school basement memorizing the Constitution, the debating team, Jim Crow discussions, and that night at the Oxford movie theater—all pointed in one direction. To his father's delight, Thurgood Marshall decided to attend law school after college.

In 1930 Thurgood graduated from Lincoln with honors in American literature and philosophy. To earn money for law school, he worked as an insurance agent, then waited tables at the Gibson Island Club. The young couple moved in with Thurgood's parents to save money. Buster found another secretarial job.

The Marshalls lived about ten minutes by trolley from the University of Maryland's law school. Tuition there was low enough that Thurgood could afford it, and he knew the school would prepare him well for practicing law in Maryland. But everyone Thurgood consulted told him the University of Maryland would never admit a black student. Thurgood was furious. He reluctantly applied instead to the law school at Howard University in Washington, D.C. Howard was a school originally opened for freed slaves. Its law school had a poor reputation, however, because until 1929, it had only a part-time evening program. It also did not meet standards set by the Association of American Law Schools.

Money was short, and Thurgood thought he would have to work for a year before starting at Howard. But his mother pawned her engagement ring, and probably her wedding ring, to help with expenses.

Thurgood was accepted at Howard. When classes started in the fall of 1930, he arose before dawn to

Howard University, Washington, D.C.

take a forty-minute train ride in segregated cars to Washington, D.C., a segregated city. He attended classes in a small building near the city's courthouse. Afterward, he went back to his job in Baltimore, had dinner with his family, typed all the notes he had taken that day, and studied until midnight. The pace of the work was so hard on Thurgood that his weight dropped from 170 pounds to 130 pounds on his six-foot-two-inch frame that first year. Even so, Thurgood, at twenty-two, realized almost immediately that he had found his life's work. Practicing law was, he said, "what I wanted to do for as long as I lived."

Charles Houston, shown here in 1935, would become
Thurgood's chief mentor and a close friend.

Chapter **THREE**

THEORY AND PRACTICE

HE WAS SO TOUGH WE USED TO CALL HIM '**IRON** Shoes' and 'Cement Pants' and a few other names that don't bear repeating." That's how Thurgood Marshall described Charles Houston, Howard University law school's new vice-dean. A Harvard Law School graduate, Houston wanted to create a first-rate law school at Howard. He also expected Howard graduates to become what he called "social engineers." He hoped his students would use their law training to end Jim Crow and shape a society that provided equal protection for all. Houston wanted his students to be superior, and he pushed them to achieve. "I never worked hard until I got to the Howard Law School and met Charlie Houston," Thurgood said.

Despite the academic demands, Thurgood remained his easygoing self. His friends called him "Nogood" and—because of his long, strutting walk—"Turkie." Thurgood earned the highest marks in the class his first year and won the prized job of assistant at the school's library. He worked long hours, and the job paid well. It also gave him time to read law books and to work more closely with his professors.

When Thurgood was in his second year at Howard, one of his professors, William Hastie, asked him to help on an actual case in the North Carolina court of appeals. Thomas Hocutt, a black man, had been denied admission to the University of North Carolina because of his race. Hocutt's case involved an 1896 decision by the Supreme Court, called *Plessy v. Ferguson.* In that case, the Court ruled that the Constitution's guarantee of equal protection under the law did not apply to a Louisiana law requiring whites and blacks to sit in separate railroad cars. *Plessy* became the foundation for what became known as the "separate but equal" doctrine, in which states could legally keep races apart as long as they provided equal facilities for each.

Thurgood thoroughly researched the *Plessy v. Ferguson* decision and gathered statistics showing that the education blacks received in North Carolina was not equal to the education whites received. In fact, Thurgood's information indicated that it was woefully inferior. Despite Thurgood's efforts, Hocutt lost.

PLESSY V. FERGUSON
LEGALIZES JIM CROW

n 1892 Homer A. Plessy, who was seven-eighths white and one-eighth black, sat in the white section of a train going from New Orleans to Covington, Louisiana. Even though the "mixture of colored blood was not discernible [visible] in him," he was arrested for violating the Louisiana railway segregation law. Two years earlier, Louisiana had enacted the law. It read, in part, "all railway companies carrying passengers in their coaches in this state shall provide equal but separate accommodations for the white and colored races."

In court, Plessy argued that the Louisiana law violated the Fourteenth Amendment to the Constitution, which guarantees citizens of the United States equal protection under the law. When the judge of the local criminal court, John Ferguson, rejected Plessy's argument, Plessy sued Ferguson. In 1896 the Supreme Court ruled that the Fourteenth Amendment applied to political actions, like voting, but not to social customs, like riding in railroad cars. The Court further said laws are "powerless to eradicate racial instincts or to abolish distinctions based on physical differences."

One Supreme Court justice, or judge, disagreed with the majority ruling. Justice John Marshall Harlan wrote, "We boast of the freedom enjoyed by our people above all other peoples. But it is difficult to reconcile that boast with a state of the law which, practically, puts the brand of servitude and degradation upon a large class of our fellow citizens."

Plessy v. Ferguson didn't specifically say the Constitution allows segregation. But because the Court failed to overturn Louisiana's law, it permitted what became known as the "separate but equal" doctrine. It gave credibility to Jim Crow laws and practices that segregated whites and blacks and kept blacks in an inferior position. The *Plessy* decision was eventually overturned in the 1950s.

As Thurgood continued his law school education, he worked with Hastie and Houston on other civil rights cases and met leaders of the black community and lawyers working for the NAACP. Thurgood also liked to visit the United States Supreme Court, the highest court in the nation, about a mile from the law school.

In June 1933, Thurgood Marshall graduated at the top of his class. He passed the Maryland bar examination, which allowed him to practice law in the state. He rented a small office in Baltimore and set up a private practice. Although he wanted to become the social engineer Houston had prepared him to be, he took whatever cases he could get and made very little money. The United States was in the middle of the Great Depression, a time when the economy was so bad that many people lost their jobs and fell into poverty. Thurgood and Buster continued to live with Thurgood's parents. So did Aubrey and his wife, Sadie, their infant son, and Sadie's mother. Aubrey had a small medical practice nearby and worked part time in a health clinic. Norma Marshall ran the household. Buster held a series of jobs to help support the family. She and Thurgood tried to have a child during this time, but Buster miscarried.

Whenever Thurgood took a civil rights case, his friends thought he was foolish, because the cases were hard to win and his clients generally paid him little or nothing. Thurgood's practice grew, but he still had a hard time paying the expenses for his office. Several times, the telephone company threatened to cut off phone service because Thurgood couldn't pay his bill. Then Carl and John Murphy, who published the *Afro-American* in Baltimore, hired Thurgood to do the legal work for their newspaper. Finally Thurgood had a client that could pay well for his services.

Thurgood became involved with several black organizations in his community, and was hired to represent the Baltimore chapter of the NAACP. In 1934 the chapter president, Lillie May Jackson, organized a boycott of white-owned stores in a shopping district near the Marshalls' home. Although most of the customers were black, store owners did not hire black workers. Blacks picketed in front of the stores and urged black customers to stay away. Buster joined the picket lines. Thurgood came home one day to find her bruised and crying after thugs hired by the store owners had attacked the picketers.

The store owners challenged the NAACP's actions in court. With help from his former teacher, Charles Houston, Thurgood won a ruling from the judge that blacks had a right to boycott stores that did not employ them. The store owners soon began hiring black employees.

While Thurgood was practicing law in Baltimore, he also went on fact-finding trips in the South with Houston, who had become Thurgood's mentor and good friend. The trips were part of the NAACP's strategy to use the separate but equal doctrine in the

Plessy decision to push for improving schools for black students.

By 1935 Houston had become the chief lawyer at the NAACP's national headquarters. He and Thurgood were eager to find a case that would bring the injustices of segregated education to national attention. The NAACP's strategy was to start with segregated graduate schools. Thurgood knew exactly which Jim Crow graduate school he wanted to tackle—the law school at the University of Maryland. He soon met Donald Murray, a well qualified black man whose law school application had been rejected by the University of Maryland. Thurgood was glad to have found someone who could and would challenge the racial policy of the law school he himself had wanted to attend. Murray had graduated from Amherst College and belonged to a well respected Baltimore family. Charles Houston agreed that Murray was the right man at the right time. The NAACP paid legal fees for the case and put Thurgood in charge.

In June 1935, Thurgood petitioned (wrote to ask) Baltimore city judge Eugene O'Dunne to order the school to admit Murray. Buster and Thurgood's parents sat in the courtroom and watched while Thurgood and Houston presented the case together. Thurgood and Houston cited the equal part of the separate but equal doctrine established by *Plessy v. Ferguson.* They argued that no other law school could equal the one at the University of Maryland for teach-

Thurgood Marshall, left, *confers with Charles Houston,* right, *and Donald Murray,* center, *about their 1935 case against the University of Maryland.*

ing someone how to practice law in Maryland. The president of the university admitted that the legal education Murray could get at Princess Anne Academy, a state school for blacks, was inferior. Since the separate educational facilities offered to Murray were unequal, Thurgood and Houston argued that the university's refusal to admit Murray was unconstitutional. Figuring that he would lose the case, Thurgood braced himself for a long legal battle—all the way to the Supreme Court if necessary.

THE SUPREME COURT

n the United States, there is no higher court than the Supreme Court. It is, in fact, the only court specifically created by the U.S. Constitution. Nine judges—a chief justice and eight associate justices—make up the Court. The Supreme Court is usually in session from October until June, and the justices divide their time between hearing cases and writing opinions.

Justices are appointed to the Supreme Court by the president. The president presents a nominee to the Senate Judiciary Committee, which usually holds hearings about the person and makes a recommendation to the full Senate. Once a nominee is approved by the Senate and sworn in, that person may serve for life, regardless of the political views of new presidents or senators. A president can only appoint a justice if there is a vacancy, usually when one of the justices dies or retires.

The Supreme Court has the power of "judicial review." It can look at laws or the president's actions and determine whether they conflict with rights granted to all citizens under the Constitution. If the Court rules the laws or actions unconstitutional, it can put an end to them.

Thousands of petitions are presented to the Supreme Court every year. The petitions are appeals from lower federal courts and state courts. The justices decide which cases they will consider, based on the cases' importance to the nation. When they take a case, the justices hear oral arguments from lawyers on opposing sides. They also read briefs (printed arguments) from the lawyers and other interested parties. After oral arguments, the justices discuss their opinions on the case and vote on its outcome. The majority (usually five or more) rules, and one justice writes the majority opinion. Justices might also publish opinions to explain why they disagreed with the majority opinion. If they voted with the majority, they might write a supporting opinion to bring up points not raised in the majority opinion.

To Thurgood's great amazement, Judge O'Dunne ordered the University of Maryland to admit Murray to its law school. After a dignified Thurgood had left the courtroom, he waved his arms over his head and danced around. For the first time, a court in the United States had ordered a public university to open its doors to black students.

The university appealed the order to a higher court and lost. That September Thurgood accompanied Murray to the law school. When the dean suggested that Murray sit apart from the other students, Thurgood found two white students who agreed to tell the dean that they wouldn't mind sitting next to Murray. Thurgood also helped Murray find much needed financial support so he could stay in school.

Just as Murray was starting his classes, Houston received a letter from Lloyd Gaines, another black college graduate. Gaines had been turned away from the University of Missouri law school because of his race. Thurgood prepared a new lawsuit. Newspapers and magazines began to write about the NAACP's attack on segregation in higher education. In July 1936, amid national publicity, the Missouri trial court ruled that the University of Missouri did not have to admit Gaines. The NAACP officials wanted Gaines to continue to push for admission to the law school. If Gaines didn't, the NAACP would have to start over with a new plaintiff. That would mean spending a lot of time and money preparing a new case. To keep

Gaines from quitting the fight, the NAACP agreed to pay his tuition for a graduate program at the University of Michigan.

In 1936 Thurgood and Houston again toured the South, visiting black schools, taking notes, and using a movie camera to document the terrible conditions they found. "Charlie would sit in my car—I had a little old beat-up '29 Ford [nicknamed Betsy]—and type out the briefs," Thurgood remembered. In some places, people threatened Thurgood and Houston to discourage them from revealing how bad the black schools were. In Mississippi, the state NAACP president assigned two riflemen to ride behind them for protection. Working on so many cases kept Thurgood extremely busy. "It was frustrating, nerve-racking, but so exciting that I never complained," Thurgood said.

Thurgood's private life was also nerve-racking. Aubrey had a hacking cough that had kept him home most of the past few months. William Marshall had lost his job and was drinking more than usual. Thurgood's private law practice in Baltimore was bringing in very little money. Thurgood asked the NAACP for a full-time, permanent position. In October 1936, he became Charles Houston's assistant at the NAACP's national headquarters in New York. His salary of $2,400 a year would allow him to help his family financially. Thurgood was also happy about the opportunity to focus on civil rights cases. "I felt that I suddenly had a real chance to do something to end Jim Crow," he said.

Officials at the NAACP's headquarters in New York City discuss a poster promoting racial equality.

The job offer came just as Aubrey Marshall was diagnosed with tuberculosis, a contagious and sometimes fatal lung disease. Aubrey's wife worried that she and their son would contract tuberculosis, so she, her mother, and Aubrey Jr. moved out. Thurgood faced a difficult choice. He realized his parents would have trouble taking care of Aubrey, but the job at the NAACP in New York was important to him. In the end, Thurgood's mother persuaded him to take the job.

Thurgood and Buster eventually found a small apartment in Harlem. But Thurgood made frequent trips to Baltimore to help out the family and work on cases in Maryland.

Thurgood Marshall at an NAACP meeting in Atlanta, Georgia, in the 1950s

Chapter FOUR

THE NAACP'S TOP LAWYER

REQUESTS FOR HELP FLOODED **NAACP** HEADquarters. New cases started and old ones made their way through the courts. The Gaines case against the University of Missouri law school dragged through the Missouri state courts, which eventually sided with the university. In December 1937, the Missouri Supreme Court upheld the lower state court decision. The case was taking up a lot of the NAACP's time and money. On the other hand, the organization was in a position to take the case to the U.S. Supreme Court. If the highest court in the country ordered the University of Missouri to admit Gaines, desegregation would receive a tremendous boost. Supreme Court rulings govern the entire nation and other courts have to follow them.

In 1938 Charles Houston left the NAACP, and Thurgood took over as chief legal counsel (attorney) for the organization. He was in charge of all the civil rights cases at the NAACP, but his salary rose only two hundred dollars a year. To earn extra money, Thurgood and Buster delivered groceries for a co-op market they had joined.

Thurgood, then only thirty, changed the atmosphere at the office. "It [had been] Dr. Whosis and Mr. Whatsis and all kinds of nonsense like that, bowing and scraping like an embassy scene. . . . I figured I'd have to bust that stuff up pretty quick. Believe me, I had 'em talking first names in nothin' time and no more of that formality business. I was gonna relax and operate in my natural-born way, and that's just what happened," he said. Thurgood took his easygoing style on the road, too. In Washington, D.C., Thurgood's humor was famous both at dinner parties with wealthy whites and at poker games with working-class blacks.

In November 1938, the *Gaines* case against the University of Missouri law school finally came before the U.S. Supreme Court. Thurgood argued that the University of Missouri had denied Lloyd Gaines his right to an education that was equal to that of white students in the state. In December the Supreme Court agreed. The Supreme Court ordered Missouri to admit Gaines to the law school at the University of Missouri or to immediately establish a law school for blacks that was equal to the one at the university. Missouri chose to set up a separate law school for blacks. Thurgood

Lloyd Gaines disappeared after the Supreme Court ruled in his favor.

considered the new law school grossly inferior, and he told Gaines not to enroll there. The NAACP and Missouri lawyers battled for months. They threatened each other with another lawsuit to determine whether the new law school satisfied the Supreme Court requirement.

Then suddenly Gaines dropped out of sight. Had someone paid him to vanish? Was he dead? Rumors suggested he had been paid to leave the country. Since there was no way the NAACP could force the university to admit a student no one could find, the lawsuit was dismissed on January 1, 1940.

Despite the dismissal, the Supreme Court decision in the *Gaines* case helped the NAACP wipe out Jim Crow exclusionary policies in other state universities. Thurgood still thought Lloyd Gaines should have gone to the law school that they had worked so hard to make available to him. "I remember *Gaines* as one of our greatest victories," Thurgood said, "but I have never lost the pain of having so many people spend so much time and money on him, only to have him disappear."

Most of the nation's civil rights cases were fought through Thurgood and the NAACP. About six other lawyers worked with Thurgood at NAACP headquarters at that time, and other attorneys helped, too. Donald Murray, the black man who had integrated the University of Maryland law school, volunteered his services. In 1940 Thurgood's law office within the NAACP became a separate organization, the Legal Defense and Educational Fund, Inc. The Fund, as it was called, handled the NAACP's legal work. Thurgood had hundreds of cases to manage. He also had to travel a lot to raise money for costly legal cases, meet with local NAACP officials, and investigate racial incidents.

Life for Thurgood during this time was not all hard work and harrowing investigations. When he was able to be home with Buster, the two enjoyed going to Harlem's restaurants and nightclubs. They listened to jazz greats like Duke Ellington and watched Bill "Bojangles" Robinson dance. Buster became good friends with Helen Dowling, the wife of Thurgood's college friend Monroe Dowling. The Marshalls and Dowlings often ate dinner together and played cards. Buster was also popular among Harlem's high society and enjoyed an active social life. However, she had still been unable to have children, despite help from Aubrey Marshall and other doctors.

By 1940, when Thurgood was thirty-two, the United States was preparing to fight in World War II. The government set up a draft, which required men to register with their local draft office and be available for military service if and when they were selected. Thurgood registered and kept his draft office informed of his whereabouts. He was never drafted, but he did become involved in the armed forces.

The U.S. armed forces were highly segregated. Black troops usually had the most menial assignments or the most dangerous non-combat assignments, such as loading explosives. Even though pilots were desperately needed, the army refused to allow blacks into its pilot training program. Thurgood persuaded government officials to set up a special training program for blacks at Tuskegee Institute in Alabama. These black pilots became the Ninety-Ninth Fighter Squadron. They were the first of the famous fliers known as the Tuskegee Airmen.

First Lady Eleanor Roosevelt publicly supported Thurgood's efforts at Tuskegee. She was on the board of the NAACP and supported civil rights. Thurgood admired her greatly. He had less admiration for Eleanor's husband, Franklin, whom Thurgood felt didn't do enough to help blacks in the United States. President Roosevelt's New Deal policies, however, offered opportunities for Thurgood in a roundabout way.

These are the men of the Ninety-Ninth Fighter Squadron, the first all-black outfit of the U.S. Air Force to go into action in World War II. They all attended Tuskegee Institute.

The New Deal was a group of U.S. programs and laws designed to help poor or underprivileged Americans. Over time, Roosevelt appointed five justices to the nine-member Supreme Court to replace justices who retired, giving Roosevelt's appointees the majority vote. Roosevelt appointed men he believed would favor his New Deal policies. These new justices also happened to share many of Thurgood's views about civil rights and the Constitution. When Thurgood's cases reached the Supreme Court, he felt he stood a better chance of winning with Roosevelt's appointees on the bench.

In most instances, the Court's decisions chipped away at racial discrimination. One of the most important, *Smith v. Allwright,* involved the right of a black man to vote in a Texas primary. Years later, Thurgood remembered this case as the greatest victory in his career at the

NAACP. But this Court also handed Thurgood a distressing defeat when it failed to overturn the conviction of W. D. Lyons, a black man wrongly convicted of murder.

During these years, Thurgood was working so hard as the NAACP's top lawyer that he sometimes passed out from lack of sleep. He traveled more than thirty thousand miles a year and was away from home two or three weeks every month. On long train rides, Thurgood hung out with the dining-car waiters, joking about his old job. Ever since he was a boy, Thurgood had liked trains. In fact, one Christmas Buster gave him an electric train set.

A new study in the 1940s gave Thurgood a different way to argue discrimination cases. Swedish economist Gunnar Myrdal believed segregation in the United States was costly and prevented the nation from achieving as much as it could. Using this, Thurgood wanted to convince the Supreme Court that there was no scientific basis for separating schools based only on race. If he was successful, the Court would have to overrule *Plessy*. It would be a difficult process, though. The U.S. judicial system is based on the principle of *stare decisis,* which is Latin for "to stand by things decided." Once a court decides something, it rarely "undecides" it. It will only overturn its own decision if it has a very strong reason to do so. The Supreme Court had upheld the *Plessy* decision since 1896.

In 1947, just as Thurgood started on his plan to overturn *Plessy,* his father suffered a heart attack and died at age sixty-five. The Marshalls, including Thurgood, gathered in Baltimore for the funeral.

Thurgood's first real legal attack on *Plessy* came soon after. Heman Sweatt, a black veteran of World War II, was refused admission to the University of Texas law school because of his race. Following a state court order, Texas established a law school at a vocational (trade) school for blacks. Following Marshall's advice, Sweatt refused to attend the new law school. Thurgood had presented Myrdal's study and the "separate isn't equal" argument to the Texas state courts. After the Texas courts ruled against him, Thurgood appealed to the Supreme Court.

At about the same time, Thurgood sent another appeal to the Supreme Court in a case in which the University of Oklahoma had admitted George McLaurin to its doctoral program. The university admitted him on orders from a federal court but then required him to sit in a "Reserved for Coloreds" section in class. The school also allowed him in the cafeteria only when whites were not eating there.

When these two cases came before the Supreme Court in April 1950, Thurgood argued that Sweatt's separate law school was unequal and, therefore, unconstitutional. He also argued that the restrictions the university placed on McLaurin represented a badge of inferiority that made it harder for him to learn.

Before the Supreme Court decided these cases, fifty-four-year-old Charles Houston died from a heart attack on April 22, 1950. Thurgood was distraught at the loss of his teacher and close friend.

In June the Supreme Court ruled that McLaurin's segregation handicapped him but didn't deny him any constitutional rights. However, the Court said that Sweatt's law school was not equal to the legal education whites received at the University of Texas. It ordered the University of Texas to admit him to the law school. The Court came close to saying that separate education was unequal simply because it was separate.

Thurgood was eager to challenge segregated public schools at the elementary and high school levels as well. First he had to find parents who were willing to file a lawsuit on behalf of their children. He knew that Harry Briggs Sr.—a black veteran of World War II—and his wife, Eliza, had started a lawsuit in South Carolina. On behalf of their son, Harry Jr., they demanded that Clarendon County improve its schools for blacks to equal its white schools. Thurgood asked Briggs and the other parents in the lawsuit to also demand an end to segregated schools. They agreed.

But what was the best way to show that segregated schools were harmful to black children? One of Thurgood's deputies (assistants), Robert Carter, told Thurgood about Kenneth Clark, a black psychologist teaching at City College of New York. Clark had done experiments with young black children in 1939 and 1940, showing them two sets of dolls. One set had pinkish-white skin; the other had brown skin. Most of

Psychologist Kenneth Clark, shown in 1970, frequently served as a witness for the NAACP in its cases against segregation.

the children liked the pinkish-white dolls and rejected the brown dolls. Clark concluded that black children suffered from "stigmatic injury." They had learned from their racially segregated culture that being black meant being inferior. Thurgood decided to use Clark's experiments to argue that segregation in schools increased the black children's sense of inferiority.

During preparations for the Briggs's case, Thurgood became involved in another civil rights issue. President Harry Truman had ordered the armed forces to desegregate in 1948, but racial injustice in the army continued. Thurgood had received letters from black soldiers fighting in the Korean War, which had begun in 1950. They said black soldiers were unfairly convicted of war crimes and received more severe sentences than white soldiers did. In January 1951, with the president's permission, Thurgood traveled to the war zone to investigate. He met with military officers and prisoners, reviewed case files, interviewed witnesses, and heard "one unbelievable story after another." Wearing military fatigues and a combat

helmet, Thurgood visited troops in the front lines—
and placed himself in great danger. "There was so
much sniper fire that you couldn't even go to the
bathroom without a buddy, and then one of us had to
take rifles," he said. When Thurgood returned home,
he reported his findings to President Truman and
General Douglas MacArthur. As a result, the army reduced sentences for most of the convicted soldiers.

In May 1951, Thurgood and his legal team boarded
a train heading from New York to the Briggs's trial in
South Carolina. Clark came with his dolls. At the trial,
about five hundred spectators tried to crowd into a
tiny courtroom. Many were poor people who had traveled miles in muggy, ninety-degree heat. Alice Stovall,
Thurgood's secretary, witnessed the scene. "They came
in their jalopy [old] cars and their overalls. . . . All they
wanted to do [was] . . . just touch him, Lawyer Marshall,
as if he were a god."

In court, South Carolina's lawyers admitted the
black schools were in bad shape and asked for time to
make them as good as white schools. When Thurgood's
turn came, he urged the court to strike down segregation itself. He talked about stigmatic injury. Clark tes-
tified that he had repeated his doll experiment with
black schoolchildren in Clarendon County and had
gotten similar results.

The trial took place before a panel of three federal
judges, including J. Waties Waring, who supported
civil rights and hoped this case would be a direct

attack on segregation. But Waring could not persuade the other judges, and the court decided against Thurgood, 2–1. The panel of judges gave South Carolina six months to equalize schools, and the governor started a massive program to upgrade black schools. By the time the six months had passed, Judge Waring had retired, and the panel ruled unanimously that South Carolina was proceeding well. Thurgood appealed the decision to the Supreme Court.

Another desegregation case was brewing in Topeka, Kansas. Oliver Brown, a black minister, sued the school board so his daughter, Linda, could attend Sumner School, a white school nearby. He did not believe she should have to make a dangerous trip to the black school farther away. With Thurgood's encouragement, Brown expanded his lawsuit to challenge the Kansas law that permitted school segregation. Brown lost the lawsuit at the state level, and Thurgood appealed to the Supreme Court.

Spottswood Robinson III, a friend of Thurgood who worked for the NAACP in Virginia, represented two black teens, Joan and Barbara Johns. The Johns had led a student walkout to protest appalling conditions at their segregated high school in Farmville, Virginia. Robinson and his law partner then decided to challenge the constitutionality of segregated schools in Virginia's Prince Edward County. They lost their case in lower court and appealed to the Supreme Court.

The Supreme Court decided to consider all three de-

Linda Brown stands in front of Sumner School in Topeka, Kansas, in 1964.

segregation cases at once, along with two others. One case from New Castle, Delaware, had started as a request that the school bus for white children pick up a young black girl in the neighborhood. The request grew into a lawsuit about inequality between black and white schools. A lower court ordered desegregation, but the state of Delaware appealed to the Supreme Court. A case from Washington, D.C., raised a technical question about whether the Fourteenth Amendment applied to schools there. The Fourteenth Amendment to the Constitution provides that a *state* shall not "deny to any person within its jurisdiction [legal authority] the equal protection of the laws." Washington, D.C., is a federal district but is not within a state, nor is it a state itself. If school segregation were ruled unconstitutional, would the ruling apply also to the nation's capital?

The Supreme Court justices wanted to review and decide cases from different parts of the country together. It reasoned that the issue of segregated schools was important for the entire nation, not just the South. These five cases were grouped together and given the name of the Kansas case: *Brown v. Board of Education of Topeka*. They became famous by the shortened name, *Brown v. Board of Education*.

Thurgood Marshall and John Davis represented opposing sides in the 1952 Briggs case.

Chapter **FIVE**

HITTING THE JACKPOT

THURGOOD AND HIS TEAM WORKED DAY AND NIGHT preparing for *Brown*. They did research and wrote briefs. These briefs were not brief at all, but long, detailed documents to persuade the justices to order desegregation.

In December 1952, Thurgood argued the *Briggs* case before the Court. His colleagues handled the other four cases. Thurgood seemed confident. He spoke in terms everyone in the overflowing courtroom could understand. He described Clark's experiments and said that separate public schools, whether or not they were equal, were harmful to black children.

South Carolina's lawyer for the *Briggs* case was John Davis, whom Thurgood had greatly admired since law school—when he would watch Davis argue before the Supreme Court. Born in 1873, Davis was a well respected white-haired gentleman who had presented 140 cases to the Supreme Court. Davis claimed it was too late to uproot segregation. He believed segregation was better for blacks. He also urged the Court to consider possible consequences of desegregation, including racial hostility at school.

But Thurgood made this important point in his closing remarks: "It seems to me that the significant factor running through all these arguments up to this point is that for some reason, which is still unexplained, Negroes are taken out of the mainstream of American life. . . . There is nothing involved in this case other than race and color." Racial discrimination, he reminded the justices, was unconstitutional under the Fourteenth Amendment.

The nine justices discussed and discussed, but they couldn't reach a decision. They ordered a second round of arguments for the following October to address five questions about the history and intent of the Fourteenth Amendment.

Chief Justice Fred Vinson did not favor banning segregation, and he might have been able to persuade a majority of the justices to uphold the *Plessy* decision. But on September 8, 1953, he suddenly died of a heart attack. President Dwight Eisenhower chose California Governor Earl Warren to replace Vinson. The president thought Warren probably shared his and

Vinson's views on segregation. Thurgood traveled to California to find out about Warren's views on civil rights issues. "I checked with the conservatives and the liberals, and all of them said the same thing. That the man was simply great," he said.

Arguments were rescheduled for December. Thurgood filed the NAACP's 235-page brief in answer to the Court's five questions. The Department of Justice, which was invited by the Court to participate, produced a 600-page brief that sided with Thurgood. Davis and his lawyers filed their briefs. The Court also conducted its own research. When Thurgood returned to the courtroom for oral arguments, he told the justices that the Court would have to show there were differences between the races, based on color alone, that justified educating them separately. That was the only way segregation could be constitutional under the Fourteenth Amendment, he said.

When the arguments were over, Thurgood waited five months for the Court's decision. On May 16, 1954, Thurgood was in Alabama when he received a call telling him he might want to be at the Supreme Court the next day. Thurgood caught the next flight to Washington, D.C. May 17 started out like an unremarkable day at Court. Then, at 12:52 P.M., Chief Justice Warren astonished the few reporters who were there by saying: "I have for announcement the judgment and opinion of the Court in *Oliver Brown v. Board of Education of Topeka.*"

Warren also said, "We must consider public education in the light of its full development and its present
place in American life throughout the [n]ation. . . .
Today, education is perhaps the most important func-
tion of state and local goverments. . . . We conclude
that in the field of public education the doctrine of
'separate but equal' has no place." The Court had just
delivered the death blow to *Plessy v. Ferguson.* Segregated schools were no longer legal in the United
States.

To Thurgood's surprise, the Court's decision was
unanimous. Warren, who was particularly influenced
by Clark's doll experiments, had skillfully persuaded
all his colleagues to support desegregation. Warren
also announced that the Court would hear a third
round of arguments to help the justices decide how to
integrate public schools.

After the justices left the courtroom, Thurgood
turned to his fellow lawyers and said, "We hit the
jackpot." When Thurgood recalled that day years later,
he said, "I was so happy, I was numb."

Thurgood celebrated the *Brown* decision with his
colleagues that night, but Buster was too ill to attend
the party. Busy with the intense preparations for the
Brown case, Thurgood hadn't realized his wife had become seriously ill. In fact, the couple had grown apart
and rarely spent time together. By November 1954,
Buster had grown so weak she required hospitalization. Only then did she tell her husband what doctors

had discovered months earlier. She had terminal lung cancer. Buster said she wanted to die at home. Her mother came to live with them and quickly took charge of the household. Buster's sister and father, as well as her friend Helen Dowling, who was a nurse, visited regularly.

Thurgood stopped work to be with Buster. He spent weeks staying by her bedside and caring for her. With

Following the Supreme Court decision on May 17, 1954, out-lawing segregation, Thurgood Marshall, center, *and two of his colleagues on the case, George E. C. Hayes,* left, *and James M. Nabrit, wear happy expressions.*

the strong presence of Buster's mother, however, the couple had trouble regaining some of the closeness they had once shared. Buster died on her birthday, February 11, 1955, having just turned forty-four. She and Thurgood had been married for twenty-five years. Heartsick, Thurgood felt the world had come to an end. Jack Greenberg, one of his colleagues, later said, "He lost a lot of weight, in fact so much that he looked like a skeleton, and he was really in bad shape."

After grieving for weeks, Thurgood did what he knew how to do best. He threw himself back into his work. But then a month after Buster's death, Walter White, the executive director of the NAACP, died. Thurgood's colleague and friend, Roy Wilkins, became the new executive director. They braced themselves for a strong backlash from Southern segregationists who had already angrily vowed to fight any efforts to integrate public schools.

In April 1955, Thurgood again stood before the Supreme Court in what was called *Brown II*. The justices had requested this round of arguments to determine procedures for desegregation. Thurgood wanted schools to be integrated by September 1955, but he asked the Court to order the end of segregation by the opening of school in September 1956. To Thurgood's disappointment, the Court didn't set a firm deadline. On May 31, 1955, the Court ordered the federal district courts overseeing desegregation in their areas to "require that the defendants make a prompt and reasonable start toward full compliance with our May 17, 1954, ruling. Once such a start has been made, the courts may find that additional time is necessary to carry out the ruling in an effective manner. . . . " In practice, the district courts had a lot of leeway in determining when schools had to be desegregated. Years later, Thurgood said, "I believed, and I still believe, that if the Court had said, 'This is the law! Do it now!' we would have avoided years of strife."

The public's reaction to *Brown II* was anything but lukewarm. While segregationists voiced their angry opposition to the *Brown* decisions, others in the country praised Thurgood for his efforts. One magazine even printed a children's song, set to the tune of "The Ballad of Davy Crocket," entitled "Thurgood Marshall, Mr. Civil Rights."

Thurgood believed more could be accomplished for civil rights through a series of progressive courtroom battles, rather than by attacking issues in a hodge-podge fashion. After the *Brown* decision, however, Thurgood saw a growing impatience in the nation for an immediate end to all Jim Crow practices.

On December 1, 1955—about six months after the *Brown II* decision—a black woman named Rosa Parks refused to give up her seat to a white person on a crowded Montgomery, Alabama, bus. She was arrested for breaking local segregation laws. Local black leaders planned a one-day boycott of the city's buses and asked the NAACP to represent the boycotters in court

Rosa Parks, right, *decided to remain seated on a crowded bus and sparked a new era in the civil rights movement.*

if necessary. Thurgood asked Robert Carter on his staff to handle the boycott case because Thurgood was busy with wedding plans.

In the months since *Brown II,* forty-seven-year-old Thurgood had fallen in love with Cecilia (Cissy) Suyat, a Hawaiian of Filipino descent who worked as a secretary at NAACP headquarters. Cissy was nineteen years younger and about two feet shorter than Thurgood. The couple married on December 17, 1955, and spent their honeymoon in the Caribbean.

Thurgood thought he had left behind a one-day bus boycott in Montgomery, but the boycott lasted longer than a year. Because of the boycott, Montgomery's black ministers formed an association and elected as president the new young minister in town—Martin Luther King Jr. Under King's leadership, the boycott was extended, and many people—including King—were arrested for their parts in the boycott. The association originally suggested that whites sit from the front of the bus to the middle and blacks sit from the middle of the bus to the back. But Thurgood insisted on taking the matter even further. He and Carter challenged segregated busing in court and won. Beginning

Martin Luther King Jr. with his wife, Coretta Scott King

December 21, 1956, black riders could sit anywhere on Montgomery's buses.

The bus boycott had cost the NAACP a lot. Thurgood had wanted to devote most of his efforts to school desegregation, which he considered more important. To make matters worse, an Alabama court ordered all NAACP activities in the state to stop on the grounds that the NAACP had organized an illegal boycott—which it hadn't. The ban lasted eight years before the Supreme Court reversed the lower court ruling. Publicly Thurgood had supported the bus boycott. Privately he criticized the tactics. He felt marches and boycotts would accomplish little for civil rights.

In August 1956, Cissy gave birth to a boy, Thurgood Jr. Thurgood Sr. was delighted finally to have a child.

That same year, about one hundred congressmen signed a document written by South Carolina's Senator Strom Thurmond in which they pledged to prevent court-ordered desegregation. The Ku Klux Klan, a white supremacist organization, increased its activities. Southern business leaders formed White Citizens Councils to deprive black citizens of credit and jobs if they dared enroll their children in white schools.

Thurgood had hoped to desegregate schools peacefully. In some places, progress was smooth and orderly. In others, Jim Crow customs died much harder. The worst school desegregation violence occurred in Little Rock, Arkansas. Nine black teens had been chosen to attend Central High School in the fall of 1957.

The Little Rock Nine: Top row, left to right: *Gloria Ray, Terrance Roberts, Melba Patillo.* Center row, left to right: *Elizabeth Eckford, Ernest Green, Minnijean Brown.* Bottom row, left to right: *Jefferson Thomas, Carlotta Walls, and Thelma Mothershed.*

Two Arkansas National Guardsmen, Carl Cobb, left, and D. D. Evans, stand guard at one of the entrances to Central High School in Little Rock, Arkansas.

The day school was to start, Arkansas National Guardsmen stood at the entrance to the school, ordered by Governor Orval Faubus to block the black students from entering the school. The guardsmen did nothing while a group of angry whites spat at the first of the black students to arrive and called for her lynching. When the other black students arrived at Central, they, too, were turned away by guardsmen and harassed by the mob. Eventually, President Eisenhower sent in one thousand army soldiers to escort the nine students to school and keep them safe. Army troops stayed at Central High for two months. The black students made it through the school year, but the school board petitioned the Supreme Court to stop desegregation. The Court stood firm. Little Rock then closed its public high schools. Thurgood and another attorney, Wiley Branton, went back to the Supreme Court, which ruled the closing illegal. Little Rock's public schools reopened in September 1959, and integration continued.

Amid this tumult, in July 1958, the Marshalls had another son, whom they named John. Thurgood enjoyed his growing family. He ran his electric trains with the boys and went bowling with Cissy. He still liked cooking, especially when he entertained their friends. "He finds it relaxing," Cissy once said. "Heaven knows what goes in the pot, but it comes out delicious!"

By 1959 Thurgood's Harlem neighborhood was filled with hostile supporters of black nationalism. These

THURGOOD MARSHALL, MARTIN LUTHER KING JR., AND MALCOLM X

By the time the civil rights movement was widespread, Thurgood Marshall had already dedicated twenty years to trying to gain equality through legal channels. New black leaders emerged in the 1950s to bring civil rights issues to the forefront of the nation's conscience. While Thurgood wanted equality as much as these new leaders did, he often found himself at odds with their methods.

Martin Luther King Jr. engaged wide support for the civil rights movement with his elegant speeches and peaceful protests and marches. Even though King preached nonviolence, he and his followers were frequently the targets of violence. Many protesters were arrested, which sometimes created more legal work than Thurgood's staff could handle. Scrambling to deal with the fallout from King's demonstrations took time away from Thurgood's careful plan of ending segregation in the schools.

Thurgood wondered if King's tactics were effective. King's supporters credit him with helping to outlaw discrimination and Jim Crow laws. King effectively spoke in favor of the Voting Rights Act, which kept election officials from making blacks pass tests and other obstacles before voting. He also fought for the Civil Rights Act, which gave blacks equal access to all public places. Both passed in the 1960s.

Malcolm X was another excellent speaker. He and Thurgood held very different beliefs. Thurgood felt blacks should push for the right to go to the same places and attain the same education as whites. Malcolm X fought for a separate nation of black people. While Thurgood had spent his career working within the law to enact changes, Malcolm X urged his followers to seize their rights "by any means necessary."

Black Muslim extremists were followers of Malcolm X, a minister for the Nation of Islam—a religious organization that called upon all blacks to resist dominance by whites. They would block Thurgood's path, threaten him, and taunt him for being part of the white establishment.

Around this time, in July 1959, rumors spread in New York that a white policeman had brutally beaten a black woman. In response, Malcolm X supporters called for violence in the streets. Stephen Kennedy, the city's white police commissioner, asked Thurgood to help. Thurgood investigated the rumor and learned the woman involved was not black, had not been injured, and, in fact, had repeatedly kicked the police officer in the shins. The officer was hospitalized for his injuries. Thurgood announced that the rumor was false. Black Muslim leaders were furious. Malcolm X's speeches against Thurgood became so violent that Kennedy offered Thurgood a revolver for self-defense.

But Cissy refused to allow a gun in their apartment with the children. Instead, Kennedy assigned a police officer to keep a protective eye on Thurgood in his own neighborhood.

A new era had begun. After more than thirty years fighting for justice in the courts, how would Thurgood Marshall respond to the emerging violence of the civil rights movement?

After returning from Africa, Thurgood and the NAACP often represented sit-in protesters. In this 1963 photo, angry whites harass a protester at a lunch counter in Jackson, Mississippi.

Chapter **SIX**

HIS HONOR

WHILE BLACKS IN THE UNITED STATES WERE RE-
claiming pride in their African roots, Thurgood Marshall
spent two months helping Africans achieve independence in Africa. Kenya, for example, was close to gaining
its independence from Great Britain. A leader of the independence movement, Tom Mboya, asked Thurgood to
help draft a constitution.

When Thurgood arrived in Kenya in January 1960,
several movement leaders had been arrested. Others—
including Mboya—were under orders not to hold mass
rallies. Mboya invited Thurgood to attend a meeting
in a building outside the capital city of Nairobi. About
two thousand Kenyans stood quietly in a field outside,
waiting to hear from their leaders. When a British

officer barred Thurgood from the meeting, Thurgood asked if he could at least give the crowd "one word of greeting." The officer agreed. Thurgood climbed onto an old car, then shouted in his booming voice, *"uhuru,"* which means "freedom now." The crowd cheered. Soon after, Thurgood accompanied the Kenyan constitutional delegation to a conference in London. He spent weeks working on provisions to safeguard civil rights for whites and other minorities in Kenya. Thurgood said he tried to give a white person in Kenya the same protection he would want for a black person in Mississippi.

By the time Thurgood returned home, black ministers in the United States had organized the Southern Christian Leadership Conference to work for civil rights. Their first major campaign involved sit-in demonstrations to integrate movie theaters, supermarkets, libraries, amusement parks, and lunch counters throughout the South. Despite his private misgivings about civil disobedience as a means of achieving equality, Thurgood publicly committed the NAACP to help the sit-in demonstrators—usually college students. Thurgood coordinated the dozens of lawyers who represented hundreds of demonstrators.

About this time, in August 1961, Thurgood's mother died at age seventy-four. Thurgood held a small funeral, which his brother Aubrey attended. By the time of Norma Marshall's death, Thurgood had spent nearly thirty years battling for justice from the lawyer's side of the courtroom. He was ready to turn over his responsibilities at the NAACP to someone else. He had fought hard to have rights for black citizens affirmed, and he was ready for others to usher in the changes mandated by the court decisions. "I've always felt that the assault troops never occupy the town," he said. "I figured after the school decision [in *Brown*], the assault was over for me. It was time to let newer minds take over."

John Kennedy, who had narrowly won the presidential election in 1960 with the help of black voters,

John F. Kennedy campaigns for president before a white crowd in West Virginia in 1960. Kennedy was helped by the number of black voters who supported him.

wanted to appoint qualified blacks to federal posi-
tions. Thurgood made it known that he would be interested in becoming a federal circuit court judge. As
such, he would hear appeals from cases tried in federal district court. Since federal judges are appointed
for life, Thurgood would have a steady income. He
would also be following in the footsteps of one of his
teachers, William Hastie. At the time, Hastie was the
only black circuit court judge. Attorney General
Robert Kennedy, assisting the president with appointments, instead offered Thurgood a position as a district court judge. The appointment was much lower in
rank and prestige than that of a circuit court judge. A
circuit judgeship was available, but Robert Kennedy
told Thurgood it was the district court appointment or
nothing. Thurgood chose nothing.

The Kennedys reconsidered. President Kennedy appointed Thurgood to the second circuit, which reviews
cases coming from courts in New York, Connecticut,
and Vermont. Thurgood was sworn in on October 23,
1961, in New York City, with Cissy, their boys, and
about two hundred others attending the ceremony. He
was seated on the bench only temporarily, since the
Senate had adjourned before it had an opportunity to
confirm his appointment. Southern senators on the
Judiciary Committee then stalled the confirmation
process for nearly a year. Eleanor Roosevelt was so
angry that she called it a "worldwide embarrassment."
Finally, the committee sent the confirmation to the

full Senate, and the Senate voted, overwhelmingly, to confirm Thurgood's appointment. The judgeship gave Thurgood financial security for the first time in his life and a chance to spend time with his children. He sent Thurgood Jr. (also called "Goody") and John to Dalton, a private school in Manhattan. Almost every Sunday, Thurgood was able to attend services with his family at the Episcopal church near their apartment at Morningside Gardens.

For four years, Thurgood served as one of nine judges on the second circuit. Thurgood worked hard. He heard cases involving many areas of law, not only the constitutional and civil law he had practiced for so long. He sometimes felt as though he were back in law school, researching complicated topics in corporate and tax laws. Like the other judges, Thurgood hired law students to assist him. He enjoyed their company and often invited them to dinner and a game of cards.

In July 1963, Thurgood again visited Kenya, this time as President Kennedy's representative on a goodwill tour. He traveled there a third time, in December 1963, to represent the United States at Kenya's independence celebrations. He was welcomed back to the new nation with ceremonies normally reserved for royalty. These trips were invigorating for Thurgood.

Back home, sitting month after month in his judicial robes, he sometimes missed the tension and excitement of his work at the NAACP. From the sidelines,

Jomo Kenyatta, left, *prime minister of Kenya, welcomes Thurgood to Kenya in 1963.*

he cheered the victories of civil rights demonstrators, and he was angry and appalled when racial riots ripped through cities across the nation. Some civil rights activities, like the 1965 voting-rights march from Selma to Montgomery, Alabama, left him wondering about the best way to achieve racial justice.

Thurgood continued to have an impact on civil rights as a judge, by deciding cases with an eye toward equal protection. Altogether Thurgood wrote more than one hundred opinions for the second circuit. Several of the majority opinions he wrote were later adopted by the Supreme Court and became the law of the land. The most famous of these was a ruling that said a New York county court could not try a murder suspect twice for the same crime. It was the first time the federal law against double jeopardy had been applied to local courts.

In July 1965, Thurgood received a phone call from President Lyndon Johnson, who told him he wanted Thurgood to be solicitor general of the United States. That would make Thurgood the highest-ranking black official ever to serve in the U.S. government.

About half of the cases that the Supreme Court hears include the federal government as one of the parties in the lawsuit. If Thurgood became solicitor general, he would decide which of hundreds of the government's cases each year should be appealed to the Supreme Court. He would also be responsible for arguing the government's side of those cases before the Court. With about two dozen lawyers in his office and the right to use lawyers from any federal agency, Thurgood would run the largest law office in the United States.

Thurgood had a big decision to make. If he accepted the position, he would take a cut in salary. He also risked trading a lifetime job for one that might last only a few years if the next president replaced him. Even so, he took the job. "I accepted because the president of the United States asked, and, secondly, the president who asked was Lyndon Johnson, who has demonstrated his leadership in civil rights. When

Thurgood, the first African American to become U.S. solicitor general, takes his oath in a White House ceremony in August 1965. To his right stands President Lyndon Johnson. Thurgood's wife, Cissy, and their sons, Thurgood Jr., 9, and John, 7, also witness the moment.

he asked you to be a part of what he is doing to give full equality to Negroes, the least you can do is help."

Some news analysts suggested Thurgood's appointment as solicitor general would be a steppingstone to the Supreme Court. Johnson later admitted that he had this in mind, but he did not tell Thurgood. In fact, Thurgood recalled that Johnson would repeatedly remind him not to expect an appointment to the Court.

Johnson, who had been both a congressman and a senator from Texas, persuaded his fellow Southerners on the Senate Judiciary Committee to accept the nomination. This time the Senate confirmed Thurgood's appointment without delay. Thurgood was sworn in at the White House on August 24, 1965. His brother Aubrey came, along with Cissy and their sons. At the ceremony, President Johnson said, "Thurgood Marshall symbolizes what is best about our American society: the belief that human rights must be satisfied through the orderly process of law."

At Johnson's request, the Marshalls moved from New York to a small house in the southwest section of Washington, D.C. Thurgood Jr. and John enrolled at Georgetown Day School, a private school in Washington. The boys took time off from school the first Monday in October to see the Supreme Court officially welcome their father as solicitor general.

In this new job, Thurgood could once again push for equality in America. Part of his job was to defend in Court the civil rights laws that Congress was enacting.

One important law was the Civil Rights Act of 1964, which guaranteed blacks the right to vote and equal access to such public places as motels and restaurants. Another was the Voting Rights Act of 1965, which ended Jim Crow practices that kept blacks from voting. These new laws were only as strong as the government's willingness to enforce them. Thurgood had some influence on this, too, because he could discuss civil rights issues directly with President Johnson.

On November 9, 1965, Thurgood argued his first major case before the Supreme Court as solicitor general. In Court, Thurgood spoke in a rich baritone voice. His humor often brought the justices to the verge of laughter. This case was no laughing matter, though. It involved three brutal deaths in Mississippi during 1964. Three young civil rights activists—one black man and two white Jewish men, all in their twenties—had been killed. "When I read that a police car had taken the kids to the deserted area where they were murdered, I couldn't eat, drink, or do anything," Thurgood said. Thurgood remembered how he had barely escaped a similar incident eighteen years earlier.

The Supreme Court agreed with Thurgood's argument that the deaths should not be handled as simple murder cases in the Mississippi courts. They were acts of racial terrorism that violated federal laws and required harsh penalties. Therefore, the three accused police officers and their co-conspirators were tried in a federal court. An all-white jury in the federal district court covering Mississippi finally convicted them. The case became the subject of the 1990 movie *Mississippi Burning.*

In most of the cases Thurgood argued on the government's behalf, he was glad when the Supreme Court ruled in his favor. He believed these cases increased equal justice under the law and protected the rights of individuals. They included cases involving fair housing, integration of a city park, and electronic eavesdropping by the FBI. He was particularly pleased when the Court upheld the constitutionality of the Voting Rights Act of 1965.

However, Thurgood's personal views about a case sometimes conflicted with the government's position. As solicitor general, he had to ask the Court to overturn its decision in *Miranda v. Arizona,* which limited the power of the police to question suspects in their custody. The government wanted police officers to be able to solve crimes quickly and easily. But Thurgood's experience as a lawyer told him that police officers too often coerced (forced) false confessions from suspects. He was glad when the justices, by a 5–4 majority, ruled against him.

In February 1967, Johnson appointed Ramsey Clark to be attorney general (the chief legal adviser) of the United States. To avoid any conflict of interest, Clark's father, Justice Tom Clark, announced he would retire from the Supreme Court. This left a vacant position

President Lyndon Johnson announces the nomination of
Thurgood Marshall to serve on the Supreme Court.

on the Supreme Court that Johnson was eager to fill. He wanted to put the first black justice on the Court. Thurgood's performance as solicitor general showed how competent he was, but Johnson didn't reveal his plans right away.

On June 13, 1967, Ramsey Clark told Thurgood that President Johnson wanted to see him. When Thurgood was ushered into the Oval Office, Johnson seemed surprised. Johnson chatted for a while, then said, "You know something, Thurgood? . . . I'm going to put you on the Supreme Court." Johnson told Thurgood to call Cissy, then grabbed the telephone receiver to tell her the good news himself.

Senate Judiciary Committee Chairman James Eastland of Mississippi and several other senators were angrily opposed to having Thurgood on the Supreme Court. Thurgood not only was black, but he believed in a liberal interpretation of the Constitution to advance social justice. Thurgood's opponents considered him "soft" on crime. They argued that adding Thurgood to an already liberal Supreme Court would ensure years of Court decisions that were unacceptable to them. Nevertheless, in August, the Judiciary Committee cleared the nomination, 11–5, and the Senate confirmed Thurgood's nomination, 69–11. On September 1, 1967, Thurgood took the official oath of office.

The new justice gets a last-minute checkup from his wife before
the swearing-in ceremony on September 1, 1967.

Chapter **SEVEN**

MR. JUSTICE

IN **1967,** WHEN THE SUPREME COURT RECONVENED
on the first Monday in October, Thurgood Marshall
wore the black robe befitting his new position: associate justice of the Supreme Court. In the visitors' section sat Cissy and the boys, Aubrey, an aunt, Cissy's
sister, and President Johnson. The other justices appeared from behind velvet curtains and took their
seats behind a long table in the majestic, high-
ceilinged courtroom. Chief Justice Earl Warren sat in
the center, flanked by the Court's most senior members. After Warren announced Thurgood's appointment and Thurgood took a ceremonial oath, the
newest member of the Court sat at the far left end of
the table. The other justices were Hugo Black, William

Brennan, William Douglas, Abe Fortas, John Harlan, Potter Stewart, and Byron White. Only Warren, Douglas, and Black were part of the Court that ruled in *Brown,* but the other justices generally agreed with Thurgood's views of the Constitution and civil rights.

One year later, the Supreme Court and the country experienced more change. The United States had become involved in the Vietnam War, and many demonstrators staged emotional antiwar protests across the nation. On March 31, 1968, President Johnson announced he would not seek reelection. Then, on April 4, 1968, Martin Luther King Jr. was assassinated. People in the black community reacted with grief and shock. Some reacted with violence. Thurgood remained at the Justice Department all night long, wishing there was something he could do as rioting and fires plagued the nation's capital and other cities.

In the midst of the turmoil that marked 1968, the Marshalls moved to Falls Church, Virginia, a few miles from Washington, D.C. Houses there once contained "restrictive covenants"—legal clauses—through which whites agreed they would never sell their property to someone of a different race. Twenty years earlier, Thurgood had persuaded the Supreme Court to outlaw restrictive covenants. With the move to Falls Church, Thurgood was the first black man on the block. Since Cissy was Filipino and Thurgood was black, the Marshalls were considered an interracial couple in Virginia. For over two hundred years, Vir-

Coretta Scott King, right, *her children, and other mourners at Martin Luther King Jr.'s funeral in Atlanta, Georgia, in April 1968*

ginia state law prohibited interracial couples from living in Virginia. Not until 1967, a year before the Marshalls moved, did the Supreme Court strike down the law as unconstitutional.

Thurgood liked his suburban neighborhood. He played ball with his sons, had barbecues, and steamed Maryland blue crabs for his friends, including black celebrity singers/actors Harry Belafonte and Lena Horne. Cissy managed the house and supervised the boys, who continued to attend Georgetown Day School.

In 1969 the Court finally set a firm deadline for school integration. The NAACP had sued thirty-three Mississippi school districts, which they claimed were unconstitutionally delaying desegregation. The justices unanimously agreed. Fourteen years had passed since schools had been ordered to begin desegregating. The Court again ordered the school districts to integrate, this time immediately.

In 1968 Chief Justice Earl Warren—nearly eighty and in poor health—had written President Johnson that he wanted to retire as soon as someone, another justice, could replace him. In 1970 President Richard Nixon, who had been elected in 1968, finally replaced Chief Justice Warren with Warren Burger. The new chief justice was a large man with a regal bearing whom the justices nicknamed "Imperial Burger." He redecorated the courtroom in a way Thurgood thought was pretentious. Thurgood enjoyed needling Burger when they weren't in the courtroom by waving to him and asking loudly, "What's shakin', chiefy baby?" Nixon also replaced another retiree, Justice Abe Fortas, with Harry Blackmun. As his fellow justices retired and were replaced by Nixon's more conservative appointments, Thurgood found it difficult to persuade four justices to his point of view.

In 1971 the Court had another major desegregation case. A federal district court judge had followed the Supreme Court's example and ordered the public schools of Charlotte, North Carolina, and surrounding

Mecklenburg County to desegregate immediately. To do so, the schools would have to bus about thirteen thousand students to schools outside their neighborhoods. About eighteen million children were already being bused to school, but this was the first time a federal court had ordered busing to achieve desegregation. President Nixon's solicitor general argued against the busing order. Thurgood wrote to his colleagues, "[W]hen school boards fail to meet their obligations, it is up to the courts to find remedies that effectively secure the rights of Negro children." The Supreme Court unanimously upheld the busing order.

In 1972 the Court decided a case, *Furman v. Georgia,* that involved the death penalty. After many stressful discussions, Thurgood managed to get a slim majority (5–4) to rule against the death penalty under certain conditions. Thurgood strongly opposed the death penalty. He believed it was cruel and unusual punishment, in violation of the Constitution's Eighth Amendment. He wrote a separate concurring opinion in which he said the death penalty did not prevent crimes and was used wrongly and far more often against poor and black defendants. He thought the United States should "join the approximately seventy other jurisdictions in the world which celebrate their regard for civilization and humanity by shunning capital punishment." Many scholars think Thurgood's opinion in the *Furman* case was the best he ever wrote as a Supreme Court justice.

The Supreme Court in April 1972. Front, left to right: **Potter Stewart, William O. Douglas, Warren E. Burger, William J. Brennan Jr., and Byron R. White.** Back, left to right: **Lewis F. Powell Jr., Thurgood Marshall, Harry A. Blackmun, and William H. Rehnquist.**

On October 8, 1972, Thurgood's brother, Aubrey, died of heart failure. Aubrey had been working in a sanitarium for poor patients with tuberculosis. Many times he had been passed over for promotions that went to less qualified whites. "I used to tell him to fight about it, but he was not a fighter," Thurgood said. Thurgood had advised Aubrey to return to private practice, but Aubrey said he could never leave the sanitarium patients who so desperately needed his help. Several months later, former President Johnson died. Thurgood and Johnson had remained friends after Johnson's term in the White House, and Thurgood was deeply saddened by his death.

On the day Johnson died, January 22, 1973, the Court issued its decision in *Roe v. Wade*. The ruling struck down a nineteenth-century Texas law that had outlawed all abortions, except those needed to save the life of the mother. The justices issued guidelines to balance the constitutional rights of the mother and unborn fetus, as well as the interests of society. They concluded that until a fetus was viable (could survive outside of the womb), a pregnant woman had the freedom to choose whether to have an abortion. *Roe v. Wade* was so controversial that people threatened to kill the justices. How many death threats did Thurgood receive? "More than I've ever wanted to count," he said.

At the same time, civil rights issues that seemed settled years earlier were again coming before the Court. Thurgood's more conservative colleagues began to undo much of what Thurgood and his earlier, liberal colleagues had struggled to win. When Thurgood thought a ruling was wrong, he wrote a dissenting opinion that criticized the Court's majority opinion.

In 1974 the Court heard another school busing case. The Supreme Court decided, 5–4, that a federal court could not order busing among several school districts to fix a desegregation violation in only one of the school districts. Thurgood dissented angrily. "Desegregation is not and never was expected to be an easy task," he wrote. "In the short run, it may seem to be the easier course to allow our great metropolitan areas to be divided up each into two cities—one white, the other black—but it is a course, I predict, our people will ultimately regret."

In 1976 the Court heard another death penalty case. This time, the Court decided states were free to use the death penalty. On July 2, 1976, Justice Potter Stewart read the Court's 7–2 decision from the bench. Only Brennan had sided with Thurgood's contention that the death penalty was unconstitutional. Thurgood read aloud his fiercely emotional dissent. Visibly shaken, he left the Court early that day—his birthday. Two days later he was in Bethesda Naval Hospital, having suffered a heart attack. Two milder heart attacks followed, keeping Thurgood hospitalized or at home for the next two months. Thurgood was only sixty-eight. Other justices had stayed on the Court until they were over eighty. After the heart attacks, doctors wanted Thurgood to exercise, lose weight, stop smoking, and cut out alcohol. But he found it impossible to break habits he had had for half a century.

Tension with his conservative colleagues increased.

In 1977 the Court decided the federal Medicaid program (a health plan for poor and needy citizens) would not pay for abortions for poor women. Thurgood dissented, arguing that it wasn't fair that rich women could get legal abortions but poor women couldn't. In 1978 the Court heard a case in which Allan Bakke, a white man, claimed he was unfairly denied admission to a medical school that reserved some places for minority applicants. The majority ruled that the school's racial quotas were unconstitutional. Thurgood dissented, arguing that the school had a right to correct racial discrimination.

In 1979 Thurgood's health again came under scrutiny when he fell down the long flight of steps at the Capitol building. He broke both arms. The next year, many people pressured Thurgood to retire so President Jimmy Carter, a Democrat, could appoint a younger, healthier, liberal justice to the Court before Republican Ronald Reagan assumed the presidency. Thurgood refused to step down. "I'm serving out my term," he said. "And it's a life term."

Justices William J. Brennan, right, and Thurgood Marshall in
January 1982. The two men shared similar interpretations of the
U.S. Constitution.

Chapter **EIGHT**

ON THE OTHER SIDE

BY **1980** THE ONLY MAN ON THE COURT WITH whom Thurgood shared many philosophies was Justice William Brennan. Thurgood was still the "social engineer" that Charles Houston had urged him to be in law school. He believed the Constitution should be interpreted to improve life for everyone, including those who were poor, or homeless, or even in prison. Thurgood thought the majority of the Court didn't understand the problems of minorities. The other justices, except for Brennan, had a narrower interpretation of the Constitution. Thurgood's arguments stretched the law further than the other justices were willing to go.

In 1980 the University of Maryland law school named its new library after Thurgood, but Thurgood refused to attend the dedication ceremonies. Instead, he reminded the school's dean that there had been a time when Thurgood hadn't been welcome on the campus. Thurgood did attend a dedication ceremony where a statue of him was placed in front of a new federal office building in Baltimore.

In 1981 President Reagan appointed Sandra Day O'Connor, the first female Supreme Court justice. O'Connor respected Thurgood, particularly for his work in civil rights. Thurgood disagreed with many of O'Connor's views, particularly her support of the death penalty. But she was his favorite conservative justice. Thurgood liked having someone else on the Court who had broken the all-white, all-male barrier, who was concerned about discrimination, and who appreciated his efforts to bring about equal justice. O'Connor would make Thurgood's work easier to bear.

As the decade wore on, Thurgood was hospitalized several times for viral bronchitis and blood clots. He had trouble walking, and his limbs and joints ached painfully. He had difficulty breathing. His eyes teared from glaucoma, and he had problems reading. But Thurgood never lost interest in his work.

President Reagan continued to appoint conservative justices to the bench, and the Court shifted even further from Thurgood's beliefs. Thurgood's simmering discontent erupted in 1987, the two hundredth anniversary of the Constitution. During bicentennial celebrations, people praised the nation's founding fathers.

Attorney General Edwin Meese criticized past Supreme Courts for often going against the original intent of the framers (authors) of the Constitution. Thurgood was furious with this analysis of the Constitution. In a speech that May, he said: "I do not believe that the meaning of the Constitution was forever 'fixed' at the Philadelphia Convention [where the Constution was approved]. . . . I plan to celebrate the bicentennial of the Constitution as a living document." In a television interview that fall, Thurgood claimed the Reagan administration was undoing the gains made during the civil rights era. Many people criticized the way Thurgood had talked about the president, but Thurgood didn't seem to mind.

For years, Justice William Brennan had been Thurgood's only close colleague on the Court. In 1990 he retired—to be replaced by yet another conservative justice, David Souter. Thurgood was the only remaining liberal on the Supreme Court.

By 1991 Republican President George Bush looked certain to win reelection in 1992. Thurgood was convinced Bush would control Supreme Court appointments for another four years, and he realized he could not last five more years on the Court. During the Court's last series of meetings for the 1990–1991 term, Thurgood told his colleagues he would retire. On the very next day, June 27, 1991, the Court decided a criminal case that reversed a position Thurgood had narrowly won in two similar cases a few years earlier.

Thurgood's dissent was blunt. "Power, not reason, is the new currency of this Court's decisionmaking. . . . Neither the law nor the facts supporting [these earlier cases] underwent any change in the last four years. Only the personnel of this Court did."

That day, Thurgood left the Supreme Court bench and removed his black robes. Then he sent this letter to President Bush:

> My dear Mr. President:
> The strenuous demands of [C]ourt work and its related duties required or expected of a Justice appear at this time to be incompatible with my advancing age and medical condition.
> I, therefore, retire as an Associate Justice of the Supreme Court of the United States when my successor is qualified.
> Respectfully,
> Thurgood Marshall

Thurgood called a press conference to announce his retirement. With him was a grandson, Thurgood William Marshall, whose middle name was a tribute to William Brennan. Thurgood summed up his career this way: "I don't know what legacy I left. It's up to the people. I guess you could say 'He did what he could with what he had.'"

President Bush nominated Clarence Thomas, a black man, to take Thurgood's place. Unlike Thurgood,

During a press conference on June 28, 1991, Thurgood announces his retirement.

Thomas opposed affirmative action—where employers or educators would try to fill their openings with qualified minorities—and abortion rights for women, and he supported the death penalty. Thomas's confirmation hearings dragged on for weeks due to allegations of sexual harassment. During the hearings, lawyers for Warren McCleskey, a poor black man facing the death penalty in Georgia, made a last-minute appeal to the Supreme Court to prevent his execution. They had appealed twice before to the Court and lost. Thurgood had vehemently dissented during those two decisions because he opposed the death penalty and because the case clearly showed racial discrimination.

In this appeal, McClesky's lawyers told the Court that two of McCleskey's jurors claimed information had been improperly withheld from them during the trial, and they no longer supported McCleskey's execution.

On September 24, 1991, the justices voted 6–3 to deny the appeal. Thurgood later wrote to his colleagues, "In refusing to grant a stay [delay] to review fully McCleskey's claims, the Court values expediency [quickness] over human life. . . . Executing him is unacceptable." Warren McCleskey was executed on September 25. A few days later, Thurgood announced that he would not delay his retirement any longer. When the Court met again on October 7—the first Monday in October—Thurgood's chair remained empty.

After retirement, Thurgood kept an office in the Supreme Court building. He collected his Court papers for the Library of Congress and spent time with his family, including four grandchildren. Thurgood's son John was a Virginia state trooper. He would later become a U.S. marshal, then the director of the U.S. Marshals Service. Thurgood Jr. used his law degree to work in government service rather than in a better paying private practice. When Thurgood teased his son about turning down the chance to make a comfortable living, Thurgood Jr. reminded him that "there was already one lawyer in the family who had done the same thing."

In July 1992, crowds cheered loudly as Thurgood Marshall accepted the Liberty Medal and its cash prize of one hundred thousand dollars during Philadelphia's Independence Day celebration. Thurgood had been chosen to receive the honor in recognition of his "leadership and vision in the pursuit of liberty of conscience, or freedom from oppression, ignorance or deprivation." The next month, the American Bar Association gave Thurgood its highest award.

Thurgood delivers a speech during 1992 Fourth of July ceremonies at Independence Hall in Philadelphia.

Thurgood Marshall with his grandson Thurgood William Marshall, age two

In the November 1992 elections, Bill Clinton, who had worked for civil rights as governor of Arkansas, unexpectedly defeated George Bush for the presidency. Thurgood, eighty-four, had retired just a little too soon. Remaining on the Court even one more year would have been difficult for Thurgood, however. His health was failing rapidly. By the end of the year, Thurgood was bedridden and in pain from a failing heart and perhaps from cancer. The day after Clinton's inauguration, Thurgood's heart problems worsened and he was taken to the Bethesda Naval Hospital.

Thurgood Marshall died three days later, on the morning of January 24, 1993.

More than eighteen thousand mourners filed past Thurgood's flag-draped coffin in the Supreme Court's Great Hall. His plain pine casket rested on a platform that once supported President Abraham Lincoln's body. Thurgood's former law clerks and all of the justices, including Justice Brennan, took turns as honor guard. The ceremonies in the Great Hall were those usually given to a justice. But the huge number of mourners and the outpouring of sentiment spoke to Thurgood's unique popularity and to the contributions he had made to improving America.

One of the mourners at the Supreme Court placed a copy of Thurgood's *Brown* brief by his coffin. It was a fitting tribute to a man who had tried for so long—as a lawyer, judge, solicitor general, and Supreme Court justice—to build a society based on the democratic principles of the Constitution. President Clinton and about four thousand others filled the National Cathedral for Thurgood's funeral service, which was televised nationwide. Then a private burial was held at Arlington National Cemetery.

When Thurgood joined the Supreme Court in 1967, almost two-thirds of the nation's black students were in integrated schools, thanks to *Brown*. When he died, about two-thirds of black students were back in mostly segregated schools. How hard it must have been to watch his dreams unravel!

Harry and Eliza Briggs, whose lawsuit was part of *Brown*, watched their dreams unravel, too. Their five children never went to a better school. Harry Briggs lost his job at a gas station. The White Citizens Council stopped all deliveries to the hotel where Eliza Briggs worked as a chambermaid, and the owners reluctantly fired her. The family tried farming, but banks would not lend them money to buy materials. Harry Briggs finally found work in Florida. His family barely survived back home on whatever money he could send them.

About forty years after *Brown,* Eliza Briggs said, "I just lie awake some nights thinking how we suffered and regretting that my children never gained a good education from our fight." But, she said, "I'm still proud that Harry stood up for justice. . . . I'd do it all over again."

Months before his death, as Thurgood Marshall received the Liberty Medal, he asked his audience to continue what he and people like Harry and Eliza Briggs had started. "I wish I could say that America has come to appreciate diversity and to see and accept similarity. But as I look around, I see not a nation of unity but of division—Afro and white, indigenous and immigrant, rich and poor, educated and illiterate. . . . But there is a price to be paid for division and isolation. . . . Democracy cannot flourish amid fear. Liberty cannot bloom amid hate. Justice cannot take root amid rage. . . . The legal system can force open doors,

On January 27, 1993, Justice Thurgood Marshall's casket was set on the Lincoln Catafalque (platform) in the Great Hall of the Supreme Court.

and, sometimes, even knock down walls. But it cannot build bridges. That job belongs to you and me. . . . We will only attain freedom if we learn to appreciate what is different and muster the courage to discover what is fundamentally the same. Take a chance, won't you? Knock down the fences that divide. Tear apart the walls that imprison. Reach out; freedom lies just on the other side."

SOURCES

7   Carl T. Rowan, *Dream Makers, Dream Breakers: The World of Justice Thurgood Marshall* (Boston: Little, Brown and Company, 1993), 109.

9   James Haskins, *Thurgood Marshall: Life for Justice* (New York: Henry Holt and Company, 1992), 69.

10 Rowan, 109; Thurgood Marshall, "Reminiscences of Thurgood Marshall," transcript of interview by Oral History Research Center (New York: Columbia University), #1736, 19; Ibid.; Ibid., #1595, session I, 33.

16 Marshall, "Reminiscences," #1595, session I, 1.

17 "Mr. Justice Marshall," *Newsweek* (June 26, 1967), 35.

18 Ibid.

19 Marshall, "Reminiscences," #1595, session I, 2.

21 "The Tension of Change," *Time* (September 19, 1955), 24.

23 Haskins, 2–3.

24 Marshall, "Reminiscences," #1595, session 1, 5.

25 Juan Williams, *Thurgood Marshall: American Revolutionary* (New York: Times Books, 1998), 49.

27 Michael D. Davis and Hunter R. Clark, *Thurgood Marshall: Warrior at the Bar, Rebel on the Bench* (New York: Birch Lane Press, 1992), 48.

29 Davis, 55; Rowan, 68.

31 *Plessy v. Ferguson*, 163 U.S. 537 (1896), 538; 540; 550; 562.

38 Haskins, 47; Rowan, 71; Ibid., 70.

42 Haskins, 47–48.

44 Rowan, 78.

50 Howard Ball, *A Defiant Life: Thurgood Marshall and the Persistence of Racism in America* (New York: Crown Publishers, 1998), 111.

51 Haskins, 73; Williams, 201.

53 United States Constitution, amend. 14, sec. 1.

56 Davis, 164.

57 Williams, 221–222; Rowan, 216.

58 *Brown v. Board of Education of Topeka, Kansas*, 347 U.S. 483 (1954), 492–493, 495.

59 John Geiger, "Mr. Civil Rights," *Pittsburgh Courier* (May 29, 1954), 13; *Time*, 27.

60 Williams, 235–236.

61 *Brown v. Board of Education of Topeka, Kansas,* 349 U.S. 294 (1955), 300–301; Rowan, 251.

67 Davis, 181.

73 Ibid., 235.

74 Eleanor Roosevelt, "The Marshall Delay," *New York Post Magazine* (August 26, 1962), 7.

79 Haskins, 124–125; "Statement of Lyndon Baines Johnson, September 14, 1965," Lyndon Baines Johnson Library, Austin, Texas.

80 Rowan, 294.

83 Marshall, "Reminiscences," #1595, session 2, 108.

88 Davis, 303.

89 Ibid., 308; *Furman v. Georgia,* 408 U.S. 238 (1972), 371.

91 Rowan, 42; Ibid., 328.

92 *Milliken v. Bradley,* 418 U.S. 717 (1974), 814–815.

93 "The Supreme Court Is a Life Term, Period," *Washington Post* (January 25, 1981), A2.

97 Haskins, 141, 143.

98 *Payne v. Tennessee,* 501 U.S. 808 (1991), 844; Rowan, 403; Davis, 382.

100 Haskins, 148; Cecilia Marshall, interview by the author (November 2, 1999).

101 Mary Gregg, Philadelphia Liberty Medal Director, unpublished correspondence with the author (May 25, 2000).

104 Rowan, 21.

105 Ibid., 453–454.

SELECTED BIBLIOGRAPHY

BOOKS

Ball, Howard. *A Defiant Life: Thurgood Marshall and the Persistence of Racism in America*. New York: Crown Publishers, 1998.

Beals, Melba Pattillo. *Warriors Don't Cry*. New York: Pocket Books, 1994.

Cavan, Seamus. *Thurgood Marshall and Equal Rights*. Brookfield, Connecticut: Millbrook Press, 1993.

Cushman, Clare, editor. *The Supreme Court Justices: Illustrated Biographies, 1789-1995* (Second Edition), Washington, D.C.: Congressional Quarterly, 1995.

Davis, Michael D., and Hunter R. Clark. *Thurgood Marshall: Warrior at the Bar, Rebel on the Bench*. New York: Birch Lane Press, 1992.

Goldman, Roger, with David Gallen. *Thurgood Marshall: Justice for All*. New York: Carroll & Graf Publishers, 1992.

Haskins, James. *Thurgood Marshall: Life for Justice*. New York: Henry Holt and Company, 1992.

Hess, Debra. *Thurgood Marshall: The Fight for Equal Justice*. Englewood Cliffs, New Jersey: Silver Burdett Press, 1990.

Rowan, Carl T. *Dream Makers, Dream Breakers: The World of Justice Thurgood Marshall*. Boston: Little, Brown and Company, 1993.

Williams, Juan. *Eyes on the Prize: America's Civil Rights Years, 1954-1965*. New York: Viking Penguin, 1987.

———. *Thurgood Marshall: American Revolutionary*. New York: Times Books, 1998.

NEWSPAPER AND MAGAZINE ARTICLES

Greene, Meg. "Charles Alfred Anderson: 'Keep 'em Flying'." *Cobblestone*, February 1997, 12–15.

Greenhouse, Linda. "Ex-Justice Thurgood Marshall Dies at 84," *The New York Times*, January 25, 1993, A1+.

Kennedy, Randall. "Fanfare for an Uncommon Man." *Time,* February 8, 1993, 32–33.

"Little Rock Case Heard in Appeal; Ruling in 2 Weeks." *The New York Times,* August 5, 1958, 1+.

"Mr. Justice Marshall," *Newsweek,* June 26, 1967, 34–36.

"The Tension of Change." *Time,* September 19, 1955, 23–27.

Williams, Juan. "The Case for Thurgood Marshall." *Washington Post Magazine,* February 14, 1999, 16+.

ELECTRONIC MEDIA

About Lincoln University, <http://www.lincoln.edu/about> (September 30, 1999).

INTERVIEWS

Cecilia Marshall, conversation with author, November 2, 1999.

Thurgood Marshall, "Reminiscences of Thurgood Marshall." Transcript of interview by Oral History Research Center. New York: Columbia University, 1977.

INDEX

OTHER TITLES FROM LERNER AND A&E®:

Arthur Ashe
Bill Gates
Bruce Lee
Carl Sagan
Chief Crazy Horse
Christopher Reeve
Edgar Allan Poe
Eleanor Roosevelt
George Lucas
Gloria Estefan
Jack London
Jacques Cousteau
Jane Austen
Jesse Owens
Jesse Ventura
Jimi Hendrix
John Glenn
Latin Sensations

Legends of Dracula
Legends of Santa Claus
Louisa May Alcott
Madeleine Albright
Mark Twain
Maya Angelou
Mohandas Gandhi
Mother Teresa
Nelson Mandela
Princess Diana
Queen Cleopatra
Queen Latifah
Rosie O'Donnell
Saint Joan of Arc
Wilma Rudolph
Women in Space
Women of the Wild West

ABOUT THE AUTHOR

Ruth Tenzer Feldman is an award-winning author whose work has been published in the United States, Canada, and France. She holds a Juris Doctor from American University's Washington College of Law. Before writing full-time, Ruth was a legislative attorney for the U.S. Department of Education. She enjoys reading, traveling, practicing yoga, writing song parodies, and visiting libraries. Ruth's husband and corgi keep her company in Bethesda, Maryland, and two grown sons live nearby.

PHOTO ACKNOWLEDGMENTS

The images in this book are used with the permission of: © Sam Falk/New York Times Co./Archive Photos, p. 2; © John Vachon/Schomburg Center for Research in Black Culture, p. 6; © Collection of the Supreme Court of the United States, pp. 12, 18; © Courtesy, Mrs. Thurgood Marshall, pp. 15 (left), 15 (right), 23; © Langston Hughes Memorial Library, Lincoln, PA, p. 20; © Moorland-Spingarn Research Center, Howard University, p. 27; © Bettmann/Corbis, pp. 28, 40, 43, 50, 62, 63, 70, 90, 94; © Corbis, p. 35; © Library of Congress, p. 39; © AP Wide World Photos/USAAF, p. 46; © AP Wide World Photos, pp. 53, 59, 66, 76, 82, 99, 101, 102, 105; © UPI/Corbis-Bettmann, pp. 54, 78, 84; © Schomburg Center for Research in Black Culture, p. 65; © John F. Kennedy Library, p. 73; © Everett Collection, p. 87; Ruth Simon/courtesy of the author, p. 112.

Front cover courtesy of © Bettmann/Corbis
Back cover courtesy of © Corbis